vodka

vodka

invigorating vodka cocktails

Bath · New York · Singapore · Hong Kong · Cologne · Delhi · Melbourne

First published by Parragon in 2007

Parragon
Queen Street House
4 Queen Street
Bath BA1 1HE

Designed by Talking Design
Photography by Mike Cooper
Introduction text and additional recipes by Linda Doeser
Food Styling by Lincoln Jefferson and Carole Handslip

ISBN 978-1-4054-9512-7

Printed in China

WARNING
Recipes containing raw eggs are not suitable for convalescents, the
elderly, or pregnant women. Please consume alcohol responsibly.

CONTENTS

introduction

Vodka is versatile, combining well with lots of mixers and juices, and the introduction of flavored vodkas has vastly increased the repertoire of contemporary cocktails. Making cocktails isn't difficult and is great fun. Reading the following guidelines should guarantee you have all the skills of a professional bartender at your fingertips.

Bar Essentials

Cocktail shaker The standard type is a cylindrical 2¼-cup container with a double lid incorporating a strainer. The Boston shaker consists of double conical containers without a strainer.

Mixing glass You can use the container of your cocktail shaker, a pitcher about the same size, or a professional mixing glass.

Strainer A bar strainer prevents ice from being poured into the serving glass. You could also use a small nylon strainer.

Jigger This small measuring cup is often double-ended. A standard measure is 1½ oz (3 tbsp). Most jiggers have a 1½-oz cup one end and a ¾-oz cup the other. If you don't have a jigger, use a liqueur, schnapps, or shot glass.

Bar spoon This long-handled spoon is used for stirring cocktails in a mixing glass.

Other basics Lots of kitchen equipment is useful: corkscrew, measuring cups, citrus juicer, cutting board, kitchen knives, citrus zester, and a blender. You will require an ice bucket and tongs.

Glasses

Cocktail glass Stemmed glass with a cone-shaped bowl (4–5 oz)

Highball glass Tall straight glass (8 oz)

Collins glass Tall narrow glass with straight sides (10 oz)

Shot glass Small glass (2 oz)

Bartender's Tips

Shaking cocktails Remove the lid from the shaker, add ice, and pour in the ingredients. Close and shake vigorously for 10–20 seconds, until the outside of the shaker is misty. Remove the small lid and pour the cocktail into the glass. If your shaker doesn't have an integral strainer, use a separate one.

Stirring cocktails Put ice into a mixing glass, pour in the ingredients, and stir vigorously for 20 seconds. Strain into a glass.

Sugar syrup Professionals use sugar syrup to sweeten cocktails. Put 4 tbsp superfine sugar and 4 tbsp water into a pan. Gradually bring to a boil, stirring. Boil, without stirring, for 1–2 minutes, remove from the heat, and let cool. Store in a sterilized bottle in the refrigerator for up to 2 months.

Chilling glasses Place glasses in the refrigerator for 2 hours before using. Alternatively, fill them with cracked ice, stir well, then tip out the ice before pouring in the cocktail.

Ice To crack ice, put cubes in a strong plastic bag and hit with the smooth side of a meat mallet or a rolling pin. Alternatively, bang the bag against a wall.

Renaissance

Cosmopolitan

THIS FASHIONABLE COCKTAIL, MADE FAMOUS BY THE TV SHOW "SEX IN THE CITY," IS THE ONLY DRINK TO SERVE AT A TRENDY PARTY!

SERVES 1
2 measures vodka
1 measure Triple Sec
1 measure fresh lime juice
1 measure cranberry juice
ice
orange peel

1 Shake all the liquid ingredients over ice until well frosted.
2 Strain into a chilled cocktail glass.
3 Dress with a strip of orange peel.

Sex On The Beach

HOLIDAY DRINKS ARE OFTEN LONG AND FRUITY AND THIS REFRESHING
COCKTAIL IS REMINISCENT OF HAPPY DAYS IN THE SUN.

SERVES 1
1 measure peach schnapps
1 measure vodka
2 measures fresh orange juice
3 measures cranberry and
  peach juice
ice and crushed ice
dash of lemon juice
piece of orange peel

1 Shake the first four
  ingredients over ice
  until well frosted.
2 Strain into a glass filled
  with crushed iced and
  squeeze on the lemon
  juice.
3 Dress with orange
  peel.

Japanese Slipper

JAPANESE BECAUSE MIDORI, THE BEST-KNOWN MELON LIQUEUR, IS
MADE IN JAPAN AND SLIPPER, PRESUMABLY, BECAUSE IT'S SO EASY TO
SWALLOW, NOT BECAUSE IT MAKES YOU SLIDE OVER.

SERVES 1
cracked ice
1½ measures vodka
1½ measures Midori
1 measure freshly squeezed
   lime juice
lime slice, to decorate
   (optional)

1 Put the cracked ice
  into a cocktail shaker
  and pour in the vodka,
  Midori, and lime juice.
2 Cover and shake
  vigorously for 10–20
  seconds, until the
  outside of the shaker is
  misted.
3 Strain into a cocktail
  glass and decorate
  with a lime slice, if you
  like.

Harvey Wallbanger

THIS WELL-KNOWN CONTEMPORARY CLASSIC COCKTAIL IS A GREAT
PARTY DRINK—MIX IT STRONG AT FIRST, THEN WEAKER AS THE EVENING
GOES BY—OR WITHOUT ALCOHOL FOR DRIVERS AND NO ONE WOULD
KNOW...!

SERVES 1
ice cubes
3 measures vodka
8 measures orange juice
2 tsp Galliano
cherry and slice of orange

1 Half fill a tall glass
with ice, pour vodka
and orange over the
ice cubes, and float
Galliano on top.

2 Garnish with a cherry
and slice of orange.

3 For a warming variant,
mix a splash of ginger
wine with the vodka
and orange.

Bloody Mary

THIS CLASSIC COCKTAIL WAS INVENTED IN 1921 AT THE LEGENDARY
HARRY'S BAR IN PARIS. THERE ARE NUMEROUS VERSIONS—SOME MUCH
HOTTER AND SPICIER. INGREDIENTS MAY INCLUDE HORSERADISH SAUCE
IN ADDITION TO OR INSTEAD OF TABASCO SAUCE.

SERVES 1
dash of Worcestershire sauce
dash of Tabasco sauce
cracked ice cubes
2 measures vodka
splash of dry sherry
6 measures tomato juice
juice of ½ lemon
pinch of celery salt
pinch of cayenne pepper
celery stick with leaves
slice of lemon

1 Dash the
   Worcestershire sauce
   and Tabasco sauce
   over ice in a shaker and
   add the vodka, splash
   of dry sherry, tomato
   juice, and lemon juice.
2 Shake vigorously until
   frosted.
3 Strain into a tall chilled
   glass, add a pinch
   of celery salt and a
   pinch of cayenne and
   decorate with a celery
   stick and a slice of
   lemon.

Mudslide

DESPITE ITS OMINOUS SOUNDING NAME, THIS IS A RICHLY FLAVOURED
CREAMY CONCOCTION THAT IS DELICIOUS WHATEVER THE WEATHER.

SERVES 1
1½ measures Kahlúa
1½ measures Baileys Irish
  Cream
1½ measures vodka
cracked ice cubes

1 Shake the Kahlúa,
  Baileys Irish Cream and
  vodka vigorously over
  ice until well frosted.
2 Strain into a chilled
  glass.

Screwdriver

ALWAYS USE FRESHLY SQUEEZED ORANGE JUICE TO MAKE THIS
REFRESHING COCKTAIL—IT'S JUST NOT THE SAME WITH BOTTLED JUICE.
THIS SIMPLE, CLASSIC COCKTAIL HAS GIVEN RISE TO NUMEROUS AND
INCREASINGLY ELABORATE VARIATIONS.

SERVES 1
cracked ice cubes
2 measures vodka
orange juice
slice of orange

1 Fill a chilled glass with
cracked ice cubes.
2 Pour the vodka over
the ice and top up with
orange juice.
3 Stir well to mix and
dress with a slice of
orange.

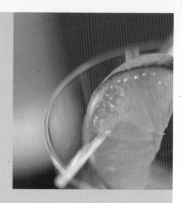

Long Island Iced Tea

DATING BACK TO THE DAYS OF THE AMERICAN PROHIBITION WHEN IT WAS DRUNK OUT OF CUPS IN AN ATTEMPT TO FOOL THE FBI THAT IT WAS HARMLESS, THIS COCKTAIL HAS EVOLVED FROM THE ORIGINAL SIMPLE COMBINATION OF VODKA WITH A DASH OF COLA!

SERVES 1

2 measures vodka
1 measure gin
1 measure white tequila
1 measure white rum
½ measure white crème de menthe
2 measures lemon juice
1 tsp sugar syrup
cracked ice cubes
cola
wedge of lime or lemon

1 Shake the vodka, gin, tequila, rum, crème de menthe, lemon juice, and sugar syrup vigorously over ice until well frosted.
2 Strain into an ice-filled tall glass and top up with cola.
3 Dress with lime or lemon wedges.

Seabreeze

PINK GRAPEFRUIT JUICE IS MUCH SWEETER AND SUBTLER THAN ITS PALER COUSIN, SO IT'S IDEAL TO MIX IN COCKTAILS WHERE YOU WANT JUST A SLIGHT SHARPNESS.

SERVES 1
1½ measures vodka
½ measure cranberry juice
ice
pink grapefruit juice to taste

1 Shake the vodka and cranberry juice over ice until frosted.
2 Pour into a chilled tumbler or long glass and top up with pink grapefruit juice to taste.
3 Serve with a straw.

Blue Lagoon

LET YOUR IMAGINATION CARRY YOU AWAY WHILE YOU SINK INTO THIS LUXURIOUSLY BLUE COCKTAIL. IT HAS A REFRESHING LEMON ZING AND SPARKLE TOO.

SERVES 1
1 measure blue Curaçao
1 measure vodka
dash of fresh lemon juice
lemonade

1 Pour the blue Curaçao into a highball or cocktail glass, followed by the vodka.
2 Add the lemon juice and top up with lemonade to taste.

Black Russian

HISTORY RECORDS ONLY WHITE AND RED RUSSIANS. THE OMISSION OF THE BLACK RUSSIAN IS A SAD OVERSIGHT. FOR A COFFEE LIQUEUR, YOU CAN USE EITHER TIA MARIA OR KAHLÚA, DEPENDING ON YOUR PERSONAL TASTE—THE LATTER IS SWEETER.

SERVES 1
2 measures vodka
1 measure coffee liqueur
4–6 cracked ice cubes

1 Pour the vodka and liqueur over cracked ice cubes in a small chilled glass.
2 Stir to mix.

Anouchka

SAMBUCA IS LIQUORICE FLAVORED AND THEREFORE NOT TO EVERYONE'S TASTE. HOWEVER, USED HERE WITH A DASH OF BLACKBERRY LIQUEUR AND THE ICED VODKA, IT'S A GREAT COMBINATION.

SERVES 1
1 measure vodka, iced
dash of black Sambuca
dash of crème de mure
a few blackberries

1 Pour the vodka into a chilled shot glass.
2 Add a dash of Sambuca and of crème de mure.
3 Dress with a few blackberries, fresh or frozen.

Godmother

AMARETTO IS AN ITALIAN LIQUEUR, SO PERHAPS THE INSPIRATION FOR
THIS COCKTAIL COMES FROM DON CORLEONE, THE PROTAGONIST IN
MARIO PUZO'S BEST-SELLING NOVEL, UNFORGETTABLY PORTRAYED IN
THE FILM BY MARLON BRANDO.

SERVES 1
cracked ice cubes
2 measures vodka
1 measure Amaretto

1 Put 4–6 cracked ice
   cubes into a small
   chilled tumbler.
2 Pour 2 measures
   vodka and 1 measure
   Amaretto over the ice.
3 Stir to mix.

Russian Double

VODKA AND SCHNAPPS ARE BOTH VERY STRONG DRINKS, SO HANDLE
WITH CARE!

SERVES 1
1 measure vodka, iced
strips of lemon or orange
  peel
1 measure lemon vodka or
  schnapps, iced

1 Layer the ingredients
carefully in a chilled
shot glass, putting
a piece of peel in
the first layer. Drink
immediately.

Innovative

Woo-woo

BE SURE TO WOO YOUR FRIENDS WITH THIS REFRESHING AND SIMPLE
DRINK. IT'S ALSO GREAT FOR PARTIES.

SERVES 1
cracked ice
2 measures vodka
2 measures peach schnapps
4 measures cranberry juice

1 Half fill a chilled
   cocktail glass with
   cracked ice.
2 Pour the vodka,
   peach schnapps and
   cranberry juice over
   the ice.
3 Stir well to mix.

Moscow Mule

THIS COCKTAIL CAME INTO EXISTENCE THROUGH A HAPPY
COINCIDENCE DURING THE 1930S. AN AMERICAN BAR OWNER HAD
OVERSTOCKED GINGER BEER AND A REPRESENTATIVE OF A SOFT
DRINKS COMPANY INVENTED THE MOSCOW MULE TO HELP HIM OUT.

SERVES 1
2 measures vodka
1 measure lime juice
cracked ice cubes
ginger beer
slice of lime

1 Shake the vodka and
   lime juice vigorously
   over ice until well
   frosted.
2 Half fill a chilled tall
   glass with cracked ice
   cubes and strain the
   cocktail over them.
3 Top up with ginger
   beer. Dress with a slice
   of lime.

Fuzzy Navel

THIS IS ANOTHER ONE OF THOSE COCKTAILS WITH A NAME THAT PLAYS
ON THE INGREDIENTS—FUZZY TO REMIND YOU THAT IT CONTAINS
PEACH SCHNAPPS AND NAVEL BECAUSE IT IS MIXED WITH ORANGE
JUICE.

SERVES 1
2 measures vodka
1 measure peach schnapps
1 cup orange juice
cracked ice cubes
physalis (cape gooseberry)

1 Shake the vodka,
   peach schnapps and
   orange juice vigorously
   over cracked ice until
   well frosted.
2 Strain into a chilled
   cocktail glass and dress
   with a physalis.

Strawberrini

WONDERFULLY FRESH TASTING WITH A SMELL OF SUMMER THAT WILL TAKE AWAY ALL YOUR CARES...

SERVES 1
1 oz fresh or frozen
    strawberries
1 tbsp powdered sugar
1–2 drops fresh lime juice
splash of fraise
2 measures vodka, well iced

1 Reserve 2–3
   strawberries to add
   later.
2 Crush the rest in a
   bowl with the sugar,
   lime juice and fraise.
3 Strain well.
4 Pour the vodka into
   an iced cocktail glass
   and add the purée and
   reserved strawberries.

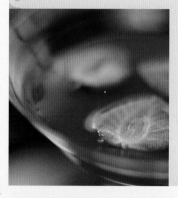

Salty Dog

WHEN THIS COCKTAIL FIRST APPEARED, GIN-BASED MIXES WERE BY FAR THE MOST POPULAR, BUT NOWADAYS, A SALTY DOG IS MORE FREQUENTLY MADE WITH VODKA. CHOOSE WHICHEVER YOU PREFER, BUT THE COCKTAILS WILL HAVE DIFFERENT FLAVORS.

SERVES 1
1 tbsp granulated sugar
1 tbsp coarse salt
lime wedge
6–8 cracked ice cubes
2 measures vodka
grapefruit juice

1 Mix the sugar and salt in a saucer. Rub the rim of a chilled glass with the lime wedge, then dip it in the sugar and salt mixture to frost.
2 Fill the glass with cracked ice cubes and pour the vodka over them.
3 Top up with grapefruit juice and stir to mix. Drink with a straw.

Blue Monday

THE LOVELY COLOR AND FRUITY FLAVOR OF THIS COCKTAIL ARE
GUARANTEED TO MAKE MONDAY YOUR FAVORITE DAY OF THE WEEK.

INNOVATIVE VODKA

SERVES 1
cracked ice
1 measure vodka
½ measure Cointreau
1 tbsp blue Curacao

1 Put the cracked ice
into a mixing glass or
pitcher and pour in the
vodka, Cointreau, and
Curacao. Stir well and
strain into a cocktail
glass.

Bellinitini

AS WITH THE BEST MUSTARD, CRÈME DE CASSIS PRODUCTION IS CENTERED ON THE FRENCH CITY OF DIJON. THIS COCKTAIL IS NAMED IN MEMORY OF A PARTISAN AND MAYOR OF THE CITY, FÉLIX KIR.

SERVES 1
2 measures vodka
1 measure peach schnapps
1 measure peach juice
chilled champagne

1 Shake the vodka, peach schnapps and peach juice vigorously until well frosted.
2 Strain into a chilled champagne flute.
3 Top up with chilled champagne.

Seeing Red

THERE IS A REAL KICK TO THIS COCKTAIL AND THE VIVID COLOR COMES FROM THE CRANBERRY JUICE.

SERVES 1
1 measure red vodka
1 measure peach schnapps
3 measures cranberry juice
crushed ice
soda water
frozen cranberries

1 Shake the first three ingredients over ice until well frosted.
2 Strain into a tall chilled glass over crushed ice, top up with soda water and float a few frozen cranberries on the top.

Raspberrini

FRESH AND FRUITY, THIS COCKTAIL IS PERFECT FOR THOSE BALMY
SUMMER EVENINGS.

SERVES 1
1 oz fresh or frozen
   raspberries
1 tbsp powdered sugar
1–2 drops of fresh lemon
   juice
splash of framboise
2 measures vodka, well iced

1 Reserve 2–3 raspberries
  to add later.
2 Crush the rest in a
  bowl with the sugar,
  lemon and framboise.
3 Strain well.
4 Pour the vodka into an
  iced glass and add the
  purée and reserved
  raspberries.

Spotted Bikini

A CHEEKY NAME FOR AN AMUSING COCKTAIL. IT ALSO TASTES GREAT, ALTHOUGH YOU MAY LIKE TO ADD A LITTLE SUGAR TO TASTE.

SERVES 1
2 measures vodka
1 measure white rum
1 measure cold milk
juice of ½ lemon
ice
1 ripe passion fruit
piece of lemon

1 Shake the first four ingredients over ice until well frosted.
2 Strain into a chilled cocktail glass and add the passion fruit. Do not strain the passion fruit, so you can still see the black seeds.
3 Dress with a piece of lemon.

Peartini

WHILE LESS POPULAR THAN PEACH OR CHERRY EAU DE VIE, PEAR BRANDY HAS A DELICATE FRAGRANCE AND LOVELY FLAVOR, BUT DON'T CONFUSE IT WITH PEAR LIQUEUR.

SERVES 1
1 tsp superfine sugar
pinch of ground cinnamon
1 lemon wedge
cracked ice
1 measure vodka
1 measure pear brandy, such
    as Poire William or Pera
    Segnana

1 Combine the sugar and cinnamon on a saucer. Rub the outside rim of a cocktail glass with the lemon wedge, then dip it into the sugar and cinnamon mixture. Set aside.

2 Put the cracked ice into a mixing glass or pitcher and pour in the vodka and pear brandy. Stir well and strain into the prepared glass, without disturbing the frosting.

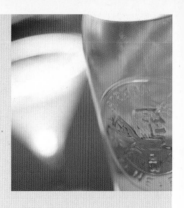

Golden Frog

AS A RULE, CLASSIC VODKA COCKTAILS WERE INTENDED TO PROVIDE AN ALCOHOLIC DRINK WITH NO TELL-TALE SIGNS ON THE BREATH AND WERE USUALLY FAIRLY SIMPLE MIXES OF NON-ALCOHOLIC FLAVORS. CONTEMPORARY VODKA COCKTAILS OFTEN INCLUDE OTHER SPIRITS.

SERVES 1
ice cubes
1 measure vodka
1 measure Strega
1 measure Galliano
1 measure lemon juice

1 Whizz 4–6 ice cubes in a blender with the vodka, Strega, Galliano and lemon juice.
2 Blend until slushy.
3 Pour into a chilled cocktail glass.

Black Beauty

FOR A VERY DIFFERENT VERSION, TRY IT WITH ONE OF THE BLACK
VODKAS WHICH HAVE RECENTLY APPEARED ON THE MARKET. THE
DRAMATIC COLOR AND SUBTLE FLAVOR ARE WORTH EXPERIENCING.

SERVES 1
2 measures vodka
1 measure black Sambuca
ice
1 black olive

1 Stir the vodka and
  Sambuca with ice in
  a mixing glass until
  frosted.
2 Strain into an iced
  cocktail glass and add
  the olive.

In Vogue

Flirtini

THIS COMBINATION OF VODKA AND CHAMPAGNE IS GUARANTEED TO
BRINK A SPARKLE TO THE EYES AND A SMILE TO THE LIPS—WHAT COULD
BE MORE ATTRACTIVE?

SERVES 1

¼ slice fresh pineapple,
chopped
½ measure chilled Cointreau
½ measure chilled vodka
1 measure chilled pineapple
juice
chilled champagne or sparkling
white wine

1 Put the pineapple and
Cointreau into a mixing
glass or pitcher and
muddle with a spoon
to crush the pineapple.
2 Add the vodka and
pineapple juice and stir
well, then strain into
a glass. Top up with
champagne.

Vodka Espresso

THIS WOULD MAKE A FABULOUS AFTER-DINNER TREAT. IT'S USUALLY
MADE WITH STOLICHNAYA VODKA AND AMARULA, A SOUTH AFRICAN
CREAM LIQUEUR WITH A CARAMEL FLAVOR.

SERVES 1
cracked ice
2 measures espresso or other
   strong brewed coffee,
   cooled
1 measure vodka
2 tsp superfine sugar
1 measure Amarula

1 Put the cracked ice
   into a cocktail shaker,
   pour in the coffee and
   vodka, and add the
   sugar.
2 Cover and shake
   vigorously for 10–20
   seconds, until the
   outside of the shaker is
   misted.
3 Strain into a cocktail
   glass, then float the
   Amarula on top.

Vodkatini

THE CELEBRATED 007 POPULARIZED THE USE OF VODKA AS THE BASE OF THE MARTINI, RATHER THAN GIN, HENCE THE VODKATINI IS NOW WIDELY ACCEPTED AS AN INCREDIBLY STYLISH AND TASTY ALTERNATIVE.

SERVES 1
1 measure vodka
ice
dash of dry vermouth
a twist of lemon peel or a
    single olive

1 Pour the vodka over a handful of ice in a mixing glass.
2 Add the vermouth, stir well and strain into a cocktail glass.
3 Dress with a twist of lemon peel or a single olive.

Flying Grasshopper

THERE ARE TWO VERSIONS OF THIS COCKTAIL—ONE MADE WITH EQUAL QUANTITIES OF WHITE AND GREEN CRÈME DE MENTHE AND THIS ONE WITH GREEN CRÈME DE MENTHE AND CHOCOLATE LIQUEUR.

SERVES 1
cracked ice
1 measure vodka
1 measure green crème de menthe
1 measure white crème de cacao

1 Put the cracked ice into a mixing glass or pitcher and pour in the vodka, crème de menthe, and crème de cacao.
2 Stir well and strain into a glass.

Purple Passion

THIS FRUITY COOLER STILL HAS QUITE A KICK AT ITS HEART. TRY USING ONE OF THE CITRUS-FLAVORED VODKAS FOR A SUBTLE CHANGE IN TASTE.

SERVES 1
cracked ice
2 measures vodka
4 measure grapefruit juice
4 measures purple grape
  juice
ice cubes

1 Put the cracked ice into a cocktail shaker and pour in the vodka, grapefruit juice, and grape juice.
2 Cover and shake vigorously for 10–20 seconds, until the outside of the cocktail shaker is misted.
3 Put the ice cubes into a chilled glass and strain the cocktail over them.

Mimi

THIS IS A DELICIOUS MIX WITHOUT THE KICK OF THE VODKA, SO MAKE A BATCH FOR NON-ALCOHOL DRINKERS AND ADD THE VODKA FOR YOURSELF!

SERVES 1
2 measures vodka
½ measure coconut cream
2 measures pineapple juice
crushed ice
slice or fan of fresh
    pineapple

1 Whizz the first four ingredients in a blender for a few seconds until frothy.
2 Pour into a chilled cocktail glass and finish with a piece of pineapple.

Metropolitan

THIS SOPHISTICATED COCKTAIL FOR CITY SLICKERS SHARES ITS NAME, BUT NOT ITS INGREDIENTS, WITH AN EQUALLY URBANE CLASSIC FROM THE PAST.

SERVES 1
1 lemon wedge
1 tbsp superfine sugar
cracked ice
½ measure vodka or lemon
  vodka
½ measure crème de
  framboise or other
  raspberry liqueur
½ measure cranberry juice
½ measure orange juice
2 cranberries, for decorating
  (optional)

1 Rub the outside rim of a cocktail glass with the lemon wedge and dip it into the sugar to frost. Set aside.

2 Put the cracked ice into a cocktail shaker and pour in the vodka, liqueur, cranberry juice, and orange juice. Cover and shake vigorously for 10–20 seconds, until the outside of the shaker is misted.

3 Strain into the prepared glass, taking care not to disturb the frosting, and decorate with the cranberries, if you like.

Greyhound

LIKE ITS NAMESAKE, THIS IS SLEEK, ELEGANT, STYLISH AND PERFECT FOR THE PURPOSE—IN THIS CASE A WONDERFULLY REFRESHING THIRST QUENCHER.

SERVES 1
ice cubes
1½ measures vodka or
  lemon vodka
150 ml/5 fl oz freshly
  squeezed grapefruit juice

1 Put the ice cubes in a tall glass and pour in the vodka and grapefruit juice. Stir well.

Bullshot

THIS IS NOT UNLIKE DRINKING CHILLED CONSOMMÉ BUT WITH A KICK. IT IS BEST REALLY COLD.

SERVES 1
1 measure vodka
2 measures beef consommé
   or good stock
dash of fresh lemon juice
2 dashes of Worcestershire
   sauce
ice
celery salt
strip of lemon peel

1 Shake all the liquid
   ingredients well with
   ice and strain into a
   highball glass with
   extra ice.
2 Sprinkle with celery salt
   and dress with a strip
   of lemon peel.

Chocolate Martini

FOR MANY, THIS IS THE ULTIMATE COCKTAIL. IT'S NAMED AFTER ITS
INVENTOR, MARTINI DE ANNA DE TOGGIA.

SERVES 1
2 measures vodka
¼ measure crème de cacao
2 dashes of orange flower
   water
cocoa powder

1 Shake the vodka,
   crème de cacao and
   orange flower water
   over ice until really well
   frosted.
2 Strain into a cocktail
   glass rimmed with
   cocoa powder.

Cranberry Collins

THE CLASSIC COLLINS DRINK IS MADE WITH GIN, BUT ITS MANY VARIATIONS ARE MADE WITH OTHER SPIRITS SO TRY THIS ONE ON FOR SIZE...

SERVES 1
2 measures vodka
¾ measure elderflower
   cordial
3 measures white cranberry
   and apple juice or to taste
ice
soda water
slice of lime, to decorate

1 Shake the first three ingredients over ice until well frosted.
2 Strain into a Collins glass with more ice and top up with soda to taste.
3 Decorate with a slice of lime.

Apple Martini

THE MARTINI FAMILY JUST KEEPS ON GROWING SINCE THE ORIGINAL
COCKTAIL WAS INVENTED IN NEW YORK IN ABOUT 1900—THIS IS ONE
OF THE NEWEST AND LIVELIEST MEMBERS.

SERVES 1
cracked ice
1 measure vodka
1 measure sour apple
   schnapps
1 measure apple juice

1 Put the cracked ice
   into a cocktail shaker
   and pour in the vodka,
   schnapps, and apple
   juice.
2 Cover and shake
   vigorously for 10–20
   seconds, until the
   outside of the shaker is
   misted.
3 Strain into a cocktail
   glass.

Crocodile

THIS IS CERTAINLY A SNAPPY COCKTAIL WITH A BIT OF BITE. IT PROBABLY GETS THE NAME FROM ITS SPECTACULAR COLOR, A STARTLING SHADE OF GREEN, PROVIDED BY THE JAPANESE MELON-FLAVORED LIQUEUR, MIDORI.

SERVES 1
2 measures vodka
1 measure Triple Sec
1 measure Midori
2 measures lemon juice
cracked ice cubes

1 Pour the vodka, Triple Sec, Midori, and lemon juice over ice and shake vigorously until well frosted.
2 Strain into a chilled glass.

Silver Berry

THIS DRINK IS PERFECT FOR ONE OF THOSE VERY SPECIAL OCCASIONS—
EXCEPT THAT YOU REALLY CAN'T DRINK VERY MANY!

SERVES 1
1 measure raspberry vodka,
   iced
1 measure crème de cassis.
   iced
1 measure Cointreau, iced
frozen raspberry, to
   decorate

1 Carefully and slowly
   layer the three liquors
   in the order listed, in a
   well-iced shot glass or
   tall thin cocktail glass.
2 They must be well iced
   first and may need
   time to settle into their
   layers.
3 Decorate with a frozen
   raspberry.

index